Feb. 8/01

To Pamela
With love & faith
that you will soon stand
in your own brilliant
light.
Gila

To Harriet Silverstein Scott
with eternal love

My admiration and gratitude to Mia Kirk and Elissa Bloom for their expertise with the production, design and editing of The Consciousness of Deserving. Most importantly, I cherish the way they took such nurturing and loving care of my book.

To David Harris, Joyce Kaiserman, Brigid Makiri, Sherri Pine and Robert Tanenbaum for their devoted consultation, editorial feedback, brilliant insight and loving support.

To Jan Salerno, there are no words to express my heartfelt gratitude and love for her extraordinary intuition and creativity in bringing a profound illumination to my words.

All of these people have woven their love through the pages of this book.

Other Books by Rusty Berkus

Life Is A Gift

Appearances

To Heal Again

Soulprints

Nell The Nebbish

In Celebration of Friendship

Red Rose Press
1535 6th Street
Suite 102
Santa Monica, CA 90401

The Consciousness of Deserving

awakening to the treasures within the mind

illustrated by Jan Salerno

by Rusty Berkus

Publisher's ISBN: 0-9609888-7-4

Printed in the United States of America

Typesetting by Abrash Typografix

Published by Red Rose Press
1535 6th Street
Suite 102
Santa Monica, CA 90401

7 6 5 4 3 2

98 97 96 95 94 93

"There is beauty in the onlyness
of our snowflake selves-
the unbeauty comes in not knowing it."

Rusty Berkus

Very few among us feel that they are entitled to a life of abundance, health, joy, creativity, harmony and most important of all, love. This is every person's inherent birthright.

You are here to have and enjoy everything. This is a logical truth. If all of us felt healthy, fulfilled, powerful and abundant, everyone around us would benefit. We could more readily use our own inner power to empower others. Our world might be a safer and more harmonious place in which to become all that we were meant to be.

One cannot claim this inherent birthright without feeling deserving of it. Your good can only be manifested in your life according to the degree to which you develop your own personal consciousness of deserving.

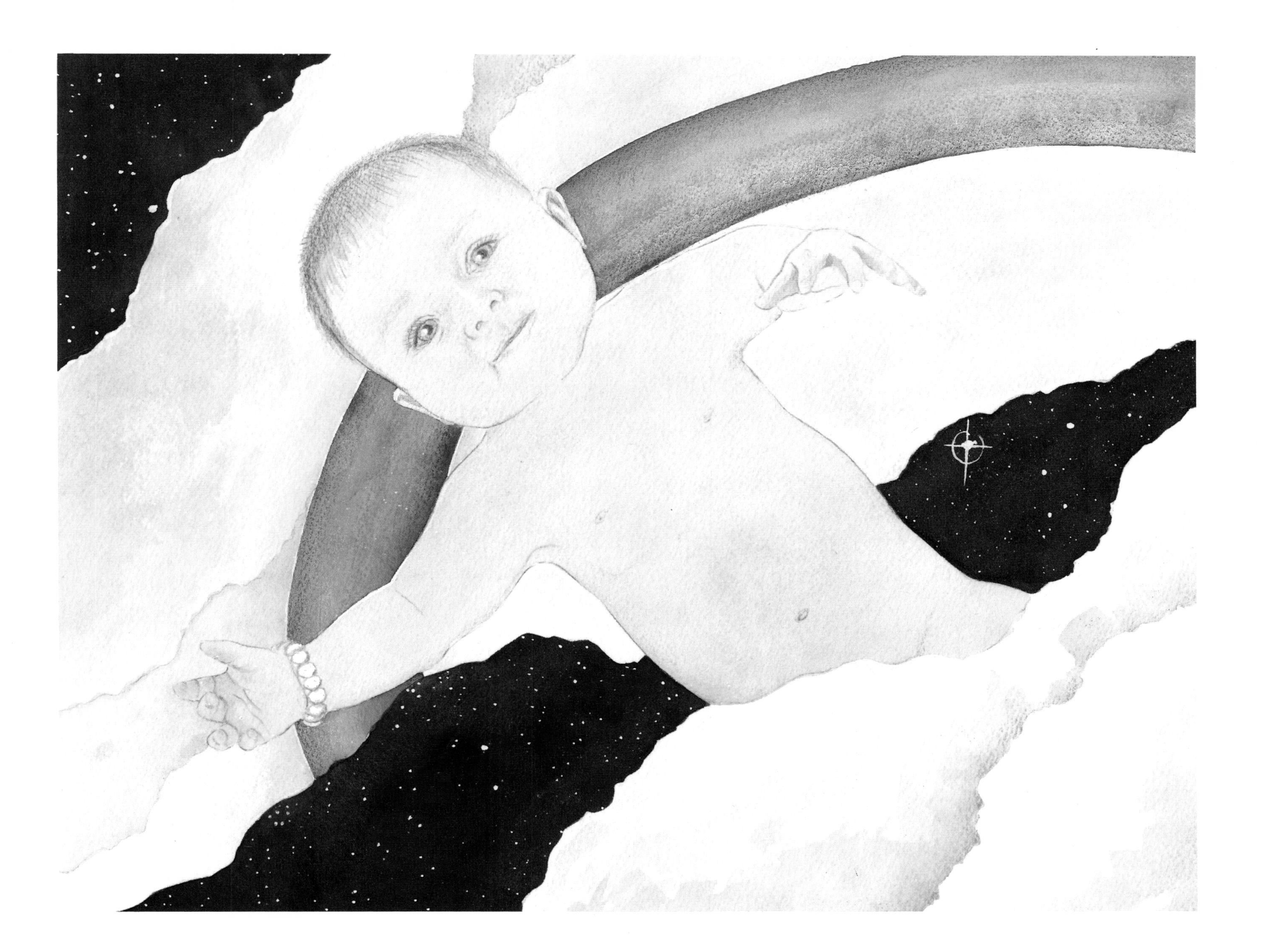

You may have chosen to believe that somehow you do not deserve these natural gifts of life. You may also believe that the good and bad which happen to you are simply due to luck or chance. This belief system does not allow you to feel in control of your destiny. It is no wonder that at times you suffer from feelings of hopelessness and helplessness.

When you lose sight of the power within to realize your good, and to restore and transform your life, you are thrown upon the sea of life without a life preserver.

There is a power within you that has love at its very core. This radiant energy is an infallible healer, and is more powerful than any other force on earth. This higher power has been given many names. Some call it God. Others have referred to it as Divine Energy, Universal Mystical Force, or Higher Self.

When you begin to put your faith and trust in this inner power, you become more awake, alive to the present moment, more open to giving and receiving love, clearing a path toward a high personal consciousness of deserving.

Some of the emotions that keep us from feeling a sense of love and deserving are fear and limitation due to the negative programming in our unconscious mind. The unconscious mind is mechanical and non-discriminating, accepting everything that is fed into it. Whatever it takes in, it also projects out into the world. If your mind is given a steady diet of negative thoughts and fears, you will feel imprisoned by your life. If your mind is filled with positive and uplifting thoughts and feelings, you will experience life accordingly.

This same principle operates on a global level. For thousands of years our world has been programmed for disease, poverty and war. This continues to be our experience.

Envision a world in which the unconscious mind is fed the truth; that we are all beings of love who deserve freedom, prosperity, health, harmonious relationships and satisfying ways to work and create in the world.

Our task is to unlearn the negative conditioning which has taken us away from our true nature and led to feelings of doubt, shame, fear and unworthiness. The oughts, shoulds and musts that rule your life are the greatest obstacles to feeling deserving. They prevent you from fulfilling your true needs and dreams, and instill a driven need to strive for perfection in all things.

This striving for perfection has reached epidemic proportions in our society. It has become a disease which destroys the psyche, just as cancer destroys our cells. This disease is called Perfectionitis. You will never find it listed in the dictionary, nor will you hear about it from the medical community. Unlike measles, which lasts only a few days, Perfectionitis continues for years and progresses into adulthood. It has many symptoms ranging from colds to cancer, from depression to anxiety. The common root is a destructive self-criticism.

One unmistakable strain of Perfectionitis is found in those people striving to be Superwomen and Wondermen. They want to be all things to all people and please everyone, but they do not know how to please themselves. Struggling for perfection, they live in fear of being exposed as human and flawed like everyone else. Often they are living their parent's dreams, following the plans and schemes of a family system whose expectations are out of harmony with their own personal hopes and desires.

Feeling cheated of their inherent birthright to be who and what they desire to be, these Superwomen and Wondermen become angry, guilty, critical and unforgiving of themselves and sometimes others. Although many of these people hold positions of power and authority, they often have underlying feelings of restlessness, unhappiness and frustration. Unaware of the source of their agitation, they labor even harder. If these feelings are habitually repressed or denied, they may appear in the form of physical or mental disorders.

Another group of people suffering from Perfectionitis are Victims and Martyrs. These people blame everyone and everything for their misfortune. Their feelings of self-pity and self-ridicule become payoffs reinforcing each other. Life becomes extremely painful and chaotic for them, and they experience great difficulty in personal relationships as well as disharmony in work and health.

People with this form of Perfectionitis oftentimes have a consciousness of lack. They sometimes live frugally and withhold from themselves and others, to the point of manifesting an illusion of poverty. They not only withhold monetarily, regardless of the reality of their situation, but they stifle the expression of their love. Living in a contracted state of loneliness, desolation and fear, they often seek out kindred souls to support and reinforce their feelings.

For those suffering from all forms of Perfectionitis, there is an underlying feeling of emptiness which often leads to addictive behaviors. In whatever way these behaviors reveal themselves, all of those afflicted with Perfectionitis have become estranged from their true nature.

Unconditional love is the universal antibody that combats emptiness, fear and other negative states which stand between us and a high consciousness of deserving.

How do you rid yourself of Perfectionitis and find your way back to the unconditionally loving essence you were at birth. You must first forgive yourself for anything you have ever done to anyone, for self-love begins with self-forgiveness. This involves accepting yourself exactly where you are in the present moment. As you move into this new mode of being, the subtle but profound shift in your thinking will free you from the grasp of self-condemnation, and allow your inner love to blossom.

It is of great importance that you not only experience continual self-forgiveness, but that you are willing to forgive others for anything they have ever done to you as well. Resentment of self and others is one of the major barriers to allowing your good to flow into your life. The desire and willingness to let go of the hurt of the past is the beginning of healing. Since your feelings and life experiences are unique to you, do not place any expectations on the timing, the rhythm or the way in which your healing unfolds.

Close your eyes, still your mind and feel the essence of self-forgiveness and forgiveness of others flow through your being. Because compassion for self is equally as valuable as compassion for others, ask for guidance in gaining greater self-acceptance in order to dissolve any and all barriers standing in the way of forgiveness.

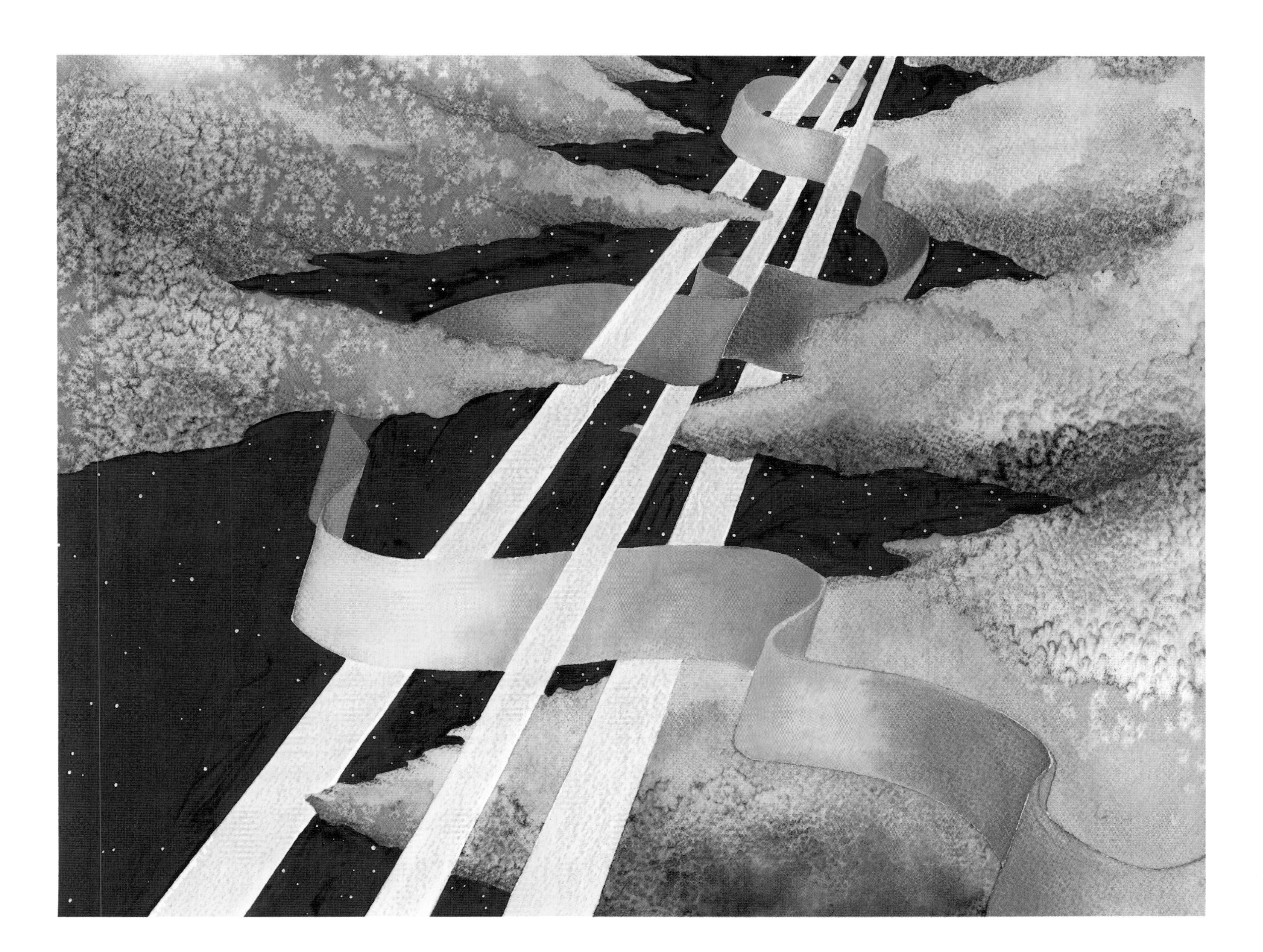

Because you possess the gift of an inner higher power that is working in your behalf at all times, you need not be overly concerned with the negative messages of your past. Most of us have not been given the gift of unconditional love. Such love embraces your shadows as well as your sunlight.

You can bestow this special gift upon yourself by focusing on what is right with you, rather than what is wrong with you.

How you feel about failure and success is of your own personal invention. Your attitudes shape the fabric of your life. It is you who has the power to accept yourself exactly as you are.

When you acknowledge who you are by practicing self-love, self-acceptance, forgiveness of self and others, you will begin to radiate an aura of dignity. Although dignity is also our inherent birthright, it has not been highly valued in the world and seems to elude us.

Think back to a moment in time when you felt beloved. Hold that vision in your mind's eye so that you can fully re-experience your own belovedness. If it is not possible to bring this state of being into memory, do not be discouraged. Emotionally embrace what it might feel like to be held dear, and how it would feel if you were able to empower another with a sense of their own dearness.

When you feel cherished and cherishable, harmony, joy, vitality and abundance are more readily magnetized to you, for fear and negativity have a difficult time finding their way into a space of love.

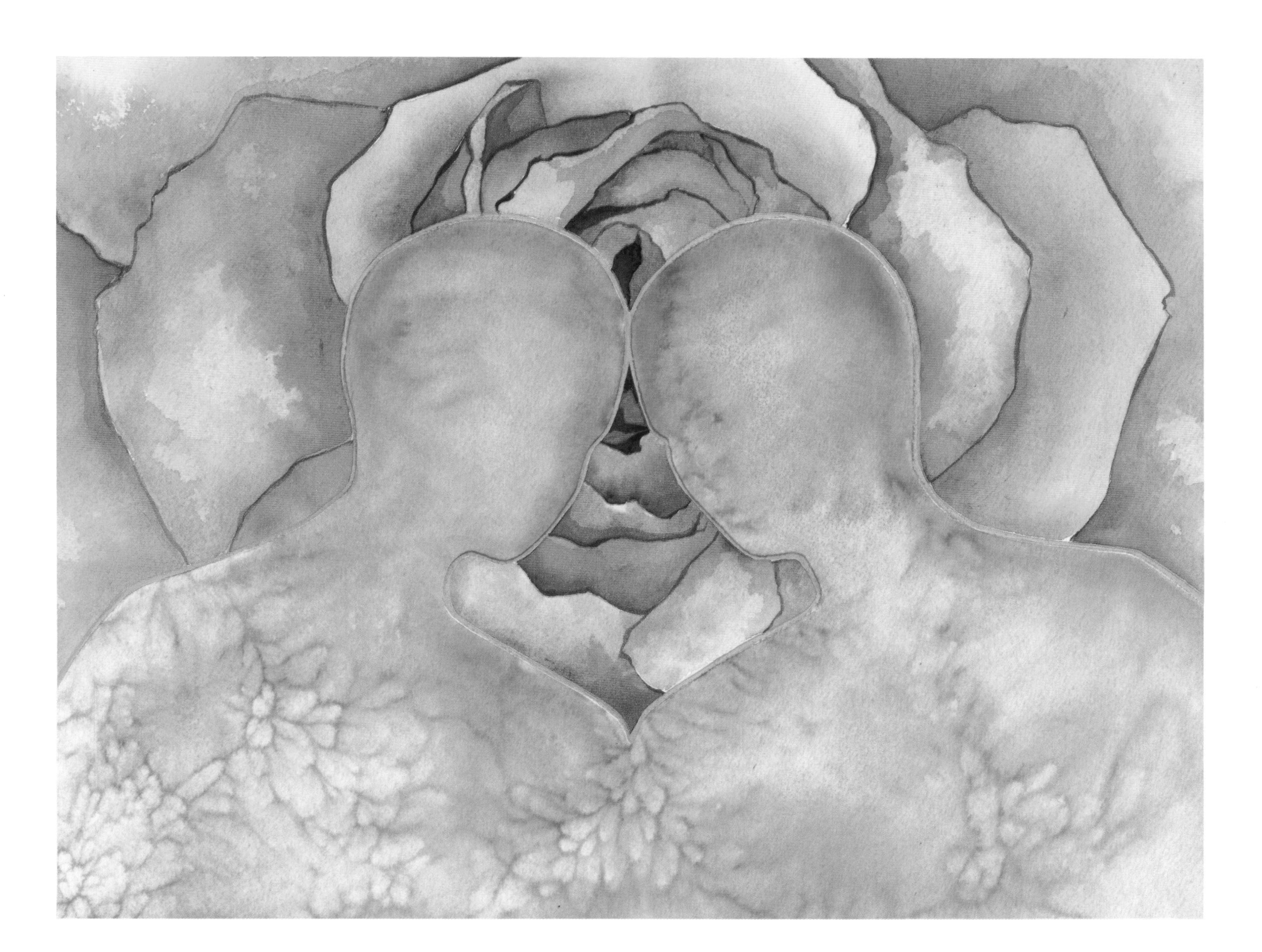

As your feelings of forgiveness continue to be depthfully affirmed, loving and healing thoughts will be planted like seeds in the newly fertilized garden of your mind. At the same time, you will discover that old negative thought-forms will automatically wither like weeds. Miracles can now begin to occur in your life. There is nothing unusual about this. It simply means that you are aligned with the natural truth of your being.

With the dawning of each new day comes innumerable opportunities to create love all around you. In the gentle act of acknowledging another, you are providing a comfort zone for all those with whom you interact.

There is a magical quality that happens between people when they feel safe in each other's presence. In a simple gesture of love, there is created a ripple effect of such profound magnitude, that it is impossible to comprehend or to measure the full extent of its power.

As you continue to practice the art of acknowledgement, and it is indeed an art, feelings of fear and competition will become a thing of the past. The truth is, there is no one to compete with and there never was. With billions of people on the planet, there is room for each one of us to be successful in whatever we do best, and to be stars in our own right.

When you look beneath appearances, you will discover that fear and competition are the products of a system which believes in lack. In reality, when you tap into your inner higher power, you will always be provided with an overflowing bounty for yourself and more than enough to share with others.

The opportunity to hear the voice of your highest self is constant once you are aware of it and take the time to listen. This voice which is sometimes referred to as the inner observer, is loving, accepting and rational. It is this still small voice within that whispers very softly at first, encouraging you to act in your own best interest. Someone may give you a book which answers a burning question for you personally. You might find yourself in another's company who wisely gives you the message you have been needing to hear.

If you do not hear these signals, the voice of your inner higher power will continue to offer you the message in a more direct way. It may shout at you through an unpleasant physical or emotional situation, so that you will sit up and take notice. If you do not heed these warning shouts, the voice will then scream at you through an even more painful experience. The same lesson will be profoundly presented to you over and over again, until the transformation that is best for your highest good takes place, and the lesson need not be repeated.

There is no time-frame for the process of inner growth. Once you have chosen the path toward a high consciousness of deserving, be prepared to receive both blessings and challenges along the way. You are here to learn your lessons in the laboratory of life. With this new self-loving and forgiving way of being, it will be easier to deal with your challenges.

As you go through the curriculum that has been especially designed for your soul, you will begin to think of the hardships, burdens and crises in your life as experiences and opportunities for growth, rather than tragedy or high drama. There will be no need to stumble around in the darkness, for you will begin to feel a sense of gratitude and an inner knowing that there is a divine presence guiding your life.

At times, you may feel yourself slipping back into old patterns of self-doubt. Endeavor to develop your inner observer. Like a nurturing parent, who is non-judgemental and rational, your inner observer reminds you whenever you are getting caught up in an old self-destructive pattern.

It is helpful to develop a sense of humor and objectivity when you find yourself enveloped by this temporary shadow. This is a natural part of the growth process and provides the opportunity to love and accept yourself in even greater depth.

Your inner observer is there to warn you before you become the star of the same old soap opera all over again. Bear in mind that this continuing personal drama has kept you from becoming all that you were meant to be in this lifetime.

Much of your pain is caused by resistance to change and the inability to accept what is happening in your life. From early on you have been taught to believe that change and growth are synonymous with fear.

In reality, change and growth do not represent fear, but rather an extraordinary opportunity to allow the good that is flowing in your direction to appear in your life. You would not have created the opportunity for change if you were not ready for your good.

It is important to know that you can develop the power and the courage to accept change. If you do not believe this is possible, you will feel that you are driving with one foot on the brake and another on the gas pedal at the same time.

It is a myth that you are put on earth to struggle. You are here to learn how to effectively meet your personal challenges, so that you can experience the harmony and fulfillment that is your inherent birthright.

Know that all things are possible when you turn your personal challenges over to your higher power. If you feel confused or doubtful about your ability to change, ask for inner guidance. Transformation does not have to be a long and painful process. If you are receptive, the way will be made absolutely clear, and healing can take place within the twinkling of an eye.

There is an essence of love buried deep inside of you aching to come forth. It is like a joyous, spontaneous child who has been locked in a cage and is yearning to be free.

As you begin to live more from the truth of your being, you will find that it takes a great deal of energy to keep the self encased in the subterfuge of repression and denial. The fruits of your inner exploration will begin to reveal themselves to you. The need for constant approval will diminish, and you will feel safer in your vulnerability. It will become difficult to operate from the limited framework of your past.

By focusing on the healing presence within, which is the logical and rational truth about yourself, the unmendable becomes mendable,and the unalterable becomes alterable.

The human organism is always moving in the direction of health. Your thoughts affect every cell, nerve, fiber, tissue and organ in your body. If you allow distorted and toxic societal messages to get in your way, you will contribute to the breakdown of both your physical and emotional immune system.

One of these toxic messages is that desiring success and feeling special and extraordinary is being selfish, egotistical and narcissistic. This is not the truth, for emptiness and frustration lead to selfishness and narcissism. Feeling good about yourself always leads to a high consciousness of deserving and affects everyone in your life in a positive way.

As your personal feelings of deserving continue to unfold, you will find yourself moving from one glory to another. The old lens of unawareness and self-doubt will begin to fade into one of self-power and enlightment. This feeling is akin to the experience of emerging from the cold shadows of Winter into the warm rays of the Summer sun.

As you go from darkness into light, you will see and feel from a new vantage point. Life will take on a lustre, vibrancy and beauty that you will have never before encountered. As you continue to heal your own personal universe, the entire planet will be uplifted.

Envision all of the energy used to create powerful military weapons being directed into planetary love and healing. In place of an arms race, there would be friendly cooperation between countries involving the quality and quantity of aid given to the hungry, the sick and the poor. The country most influential in solving major global problems such as famine, pollution and disease would receive great honor. This recognition would be a celebration of excellence throughout the world, and would encourage nations to empower each other by sharing creative ideas toward a common goal that would serve all humanity.

Let us not underestimate the power of the mind to put this global thought into consciousness.
Regardless of the diversity of our languages, customs and cultures,
we are all interconnected.

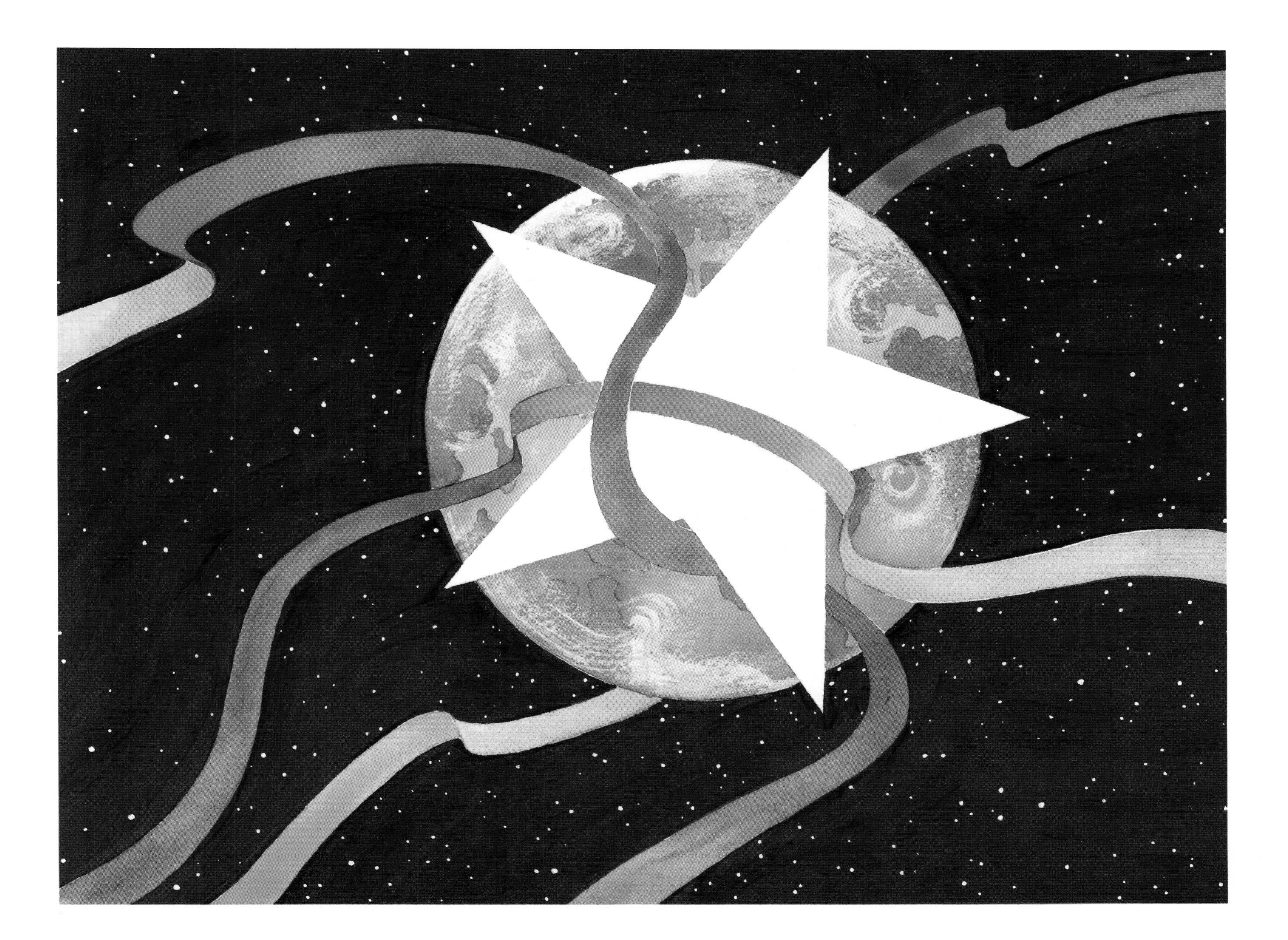

Look at the landscape of your life. Observe the quality of your relationships, your living and working environment, the experiences and situations you attract, and the way people treat you. The truth is that everything in your life is an embodiment of your state of consciousness. It is sometimes difficult to accept the fact that you are personally responsible for the quality of your life.

Putting the responsibility for your happiness on people, places and things outside of yourself is looking for treasures in the wrong places. It is a comfort to know that you have the abiltity to guide and direct your destiny by getting in touch with the gifts that lie within you.

To walk in the world with the deep knowing that you can call on a magnificent power at all times is to feel Grace. This healing energy dwells within you, always waiting to comfort you, guide you, cheer you on, and reveal one of your most sacred hidden treasures-
a high consciousness of deserving.

In order to enhance the reader's understanding, enjoyment and intimacy with The Consciousness of Deserving, both the writer and the artist want to share the language of imagery that evolved out of their creative process.

Baby	Inherent Birthright
Bricks	Prisons of the Mind, Negative Belief Systems Oughts, Shoulds and Musts, Perfectionitis
Dark Clouds	Negativity
Eagle	Higher Power, Highest Self, Inner Observer
Earth-Globe	Humanity
Goldline	Aura of Dignity
Heart	Unconditional Love
Pink Rose	The Core of Your Being
Purple	Truth, Introspection
Rainbow-Rainbow Ribbons	The Consciousness of Deserving
Spiral	Place of Radiant Energy filled with Truth
Star	Your Starhood, Your Magnificence, Your Greatness
Sun	Forgiveness, Miracles
Sunbeams-Starbeams	Positive Energy, All of your Good flowing to you
Yellow Brick Road	Path of Freedom

About the Author

Rusty Berkus is a poet, composer, lyricist and has her Master's degree in Marriage and Family Counseling. It is her belief that good is always flowing in our direction. By focusing on all aspects of consciousness that would enable us to accept our good, we give ourselves the rare opportunity to develop a high consciousness of deserving. This new way of thinking will positively affect our personal existence, and will empower all those who touch our lives.

About the Illustrator

Jan Salerno is a visionary artist, printmaker, graphic designer and mother. "Contained in this collective process of becoming whole, we are awakening to our power to reimage our world, and our planet, according to our consciousness of deserving. In gratitude we receive inspiration from our higher power and embrace the planetary healing with love and beauty."